Truck Ent Spotter

This Truck Spotting Jotter belongs to:				
Telephone Number:				
Jotter Book Number:				
From: Day		Date	Month	Year
To: Day		Date	Month	Year

Safety First

There are generally two forms of truck spotter. The casual observer who may spot certain trucks from certain companies when on a car journey or out and about. The hardened enthusiast, who thinks nothing of getting up early at the weekend and heading off to the far flung corners of the country to stake out a specific truck hot spot for some haulage action. Whichever you may be, you need to follow a few simple rules to make sure you and others stay safe.

In the Car
- If you are the driver, do not take you eyes off the road to get that elusive spot. It may be the last thing you do.
- If you are a passenger and get that elusive spot, do not distract the driver.
- Never tail gate a truck to get its number.
- Never sit in a tucks blind spot (usually by the cab) to get its name/number
- When overtaking a truck on the motorway, do so in one fluid movement. Do not sit next to the truck.
- Remember, if you cannot see the drivers mirrors, then the driver cannot see you.

Motorway Service Stations
Motorway service stations are a great place to see a whole variety of trucks parked up. However, with vehicles moving all about, there are various dangers to be aware of.

- Park your car in a marked parking bay. Remember you will typically only be allowed to park for up to 2 hours.
- Watch out for traffic and other vehicles at the services, that may move without warning.
- The use of a yellow high visibility vest is highly recommended to keep you visible and so safe.
- Do not wander in between or behind trucks. Apart from the fact that you may get knocked down, it could be construed as suspicious behaviour.
- Be courteous to others and don't get in the way of members of the public or drivers who may be passing by and not share your enthusiasm.
- Do not use flash photography. Turn your flash off.
- If challenged by authority, be polite and do what is asked.
- Walk, don't run about.

On the Roadside
If you are going to wait on the roadside either outside a depot or at another location in order to spot or get a good photo, please remember the following points:

- Park your car in a sensible place, so as you are not blocking the traffic flow or causing an obstruction.
- The use of a yellow high visibility vest is highly recommended to keep you visible and so safe.
- Stay back away from the edge of the kerb/road, out of the way.
- Be courteous to others and don't get in the way of other members of the public who may be passing by and not share your enthusiasm.

Spotter Jotter

- Be careful if using a camera monopod or tripod and not trip yourself or others up.
- Do not use flash photography. Turn your flash off.
- Do not lean or climb to see over bridge parapets to take pictures. There is a reason they are as high as they are. Faces over the tops of bridge parapets make drivers very nervous and you could fall over/drop something over onto the road below, causing an accident. Taking photos from a bridge can make some drivers nervous that it is a police speed trap.
- If challenged by authority, be polite and do what is asked.
- Walk, don't run about.
- No hi-jinx or rowdy behaviour, no matter how excited you are to get that elusive spot!
- Take your litter home with you.
- Do not trespass to get that elusive spot or photo. It is just not worth it.

Depots
If you have been granted permission to visit a depot, please follow the points below:

- Follow the instructions of your host. The instructions are for your safety and the safety of others.
- Wear Personal Protective Equipment (PPE) such as a yellow high visibility vest as required or as provided to you.
- Never wander off from the host/party if on a group visit.
- Stick to marked walking routes and do not take short cuts.
- Never cross between vehicles or behind reversing vehicles.
- Allow vehicles to pass by first, staying well back out of the way.
- If you need to pass a vehicle that has its engine running and a driver in the cab, make sure you get the drivers attention and agreement you can pass safely.
- Remember, if you cannot see the drivers mirrors, then the driver cannot see you.
- Never climb on anything including lorry trailers or steps/ladders to get a better photo, unless you have been granted permission to do.

Safety and Security
If you see anything suspicious, or require urgent Police, Fire or Ambulance assistant, they can be contacted on:

- **Emergency – Dial 999 or 112 from a mobile telephone**

The Police can also be contacted on 101 for non emergency calls.

Pictures
- ***Front Cover***: Eddie Stobart liveried Scania R440 "Blake Ellie" M468 road-train at Warrington.
- ***Back Cover – Top:*** Stobart Rail liveried Scania R560 "Angela Kay" RV317 at Carlisle.
- ***Back Cover – Bottom:*** Stobart Group liveried Scania R460 "Sienna Belle" H8243 with a log trailer at Carlisle. "Jade Cheri" stands behind – see page 1 for picture and below for details.
- ***Page 1:*** Stobart Group liveried Scania R450 "Jade Cheri" with a Renewable Energy liveried biomass "walking floor" trailer at Carlisle.

Truck Enthusiasts

Name/Fleet Number/Registration	Location	Date

Spotter Jotter

Name/Fleet Number/Registration	Location	Date

Truck Enthusiasts

Name/Fleet Number/Registration	Location	Date

Spotter Jotter

Name/Fleet Number/Registration	Location	Date

Truck Enthusiasts

Name/Fleet Number/Registration	Location	Date

Spotter Jotter

Name/Fleet Number/Registration	Location	Date

Truck Enthusiasts

Name/Fleet Number/Registration	Location	Date

Spotter Jotter

Name/Fleet Number/Registration	Location	Date

Truck Enthusiasts

Name/Fleet Number/Registration	Location	Date

Spotter Jotter

Name/Fleet Number/Registration	Location	Date

Truck Enthusiasts

Name/Fleet Number/Registration	Location	Date

Spotter Jotter

Name/Fleet Number/Registration	Location	Date

Truck Enthusiasts

Name/Fleet Number/Registration	Location	Date

Spotter Jotter

Name/Fleet Number/Registration	Location	Date

Truck Enthusiasts

Name/Fleet Number/Registration	Location	Date

Spotter Jotter

Name/Fleet Number/Registration	Location	Date

Truck Enthusiasts

Name/Fleet Number/Registration	Location	Date

Spotter Jotter

Name/Fleet Number/Registration	Location	Date

Truck Enthusiasts

Name/Fleet Number/Registration	Location	Date

Spotter Jotter

Name/Fleet Number/Registration	Location	Date

Truck Enthusiasts

Name/Fleet Number/Registration	Location	Date

Spotter Jotter

Name/Fleet Number/Registration	Location	Date

Truck Enthusiasts

Name/Fleet Number/Registration	Location	Date

Spotter Jotter

Name/Fleet Number/Registration	Location	Date

Truck Enthusiasts

Name/Fleet Number/Registration	Location	Date

Copyright © 2016 by Jon Jackson
All rights reserved. No part of this publication may be reproduced, distributed, or transmitted in any form or by any means, including photocopying, recording, or other electronic or mechanical methods, without the prior written permission of the publisher.

Published by Really Useful Publishing Company
Publisher's Cataloguing–in–Publication data
Jackson, Jonathan
A title of book: *Truck Enthusiasts Spotter Jotter* / Jon Jackson

The names and/or references to any organisation, operator, manufacturer, supplier, product, service, brand etc appearing in this book are the trademarks and/or registered trademarks of their respective owners. They are used for illustrative purposes only and do not imply any endorsement, recommendation or association.

E&OE First Edition March, 2016

ISBN–10: 1530669359   ISBN–13: 978-1530669356

Printed in Great Britain
by Amazon

58198401R00020

Series advisor:
Colin Jeal

Photographs by:
Linda Lewis
Dick Mills

Front cover painting by:
Julie Stooks

Your First

AQUARIUM

CONTENTS

Tank Size..............4	pH & Hardness ..24
Temperature 9	Feeding..............25
Air Pumps/Filters 11	Setting Up 27
Furnishings..........16	Bibliography 33
Lighting 21	

©1996
by Kingdom
Books
PO7 6AR
ENGLAND

your first aquarium

Kingdom Books is an imprint of T.F.H. Publications   Printed in England.

TANK SIZE

your first aquarium TANK SIZE

When choosing an aquarium your main consideration must be to match the aquarium to the size and number of fish to be kept in it. Unfortunately, the beginner often adds fish at random to the original setup, without realising the degree of overcrowding that is being created.

An overpopulated aquarium is one of the most frequent causes of failure in the hobby. Overpopulation stresses the fish and leads to a shortage of oxygen. Where conditions have been crowded for some time, excess nitrogenous compounds (ammonia, nitrates and nitrites) build up in the water and have an adverse effect on the fish. Plants help to clear this excess nitrogen to a considerable extent, since they are able to use nitrates, the end product of the nitrogen cycle, but even the plants will suffer when the concentration becomes too great.

Another consideration is the transmission of disease from one fish to another. Most significant fish diseases are infections of various types, and their spread in the aquarium can be extremely rapid under crowded conditions. The hobbyist must realise the remarkable difference between a small confined body of water such as an aquarium and the fish's natural habitat in a lake, stream or river. The confinement alone stresses the fish,

When setting up your aquarium do not be tempted to put in too many fish for the size of the tank.

TANK SIZE

but crowded conditions make things much worse, often leading to a decrease in the vitality and, eventually, the health of the fish.

There are no hard and fast rules governing stocking levels in the aquarium, as many factors will influence the number of fish your tank will support. The most common method of assessing the number of fish your tank will hold is a ratio of centimetres of fish to litres of water. This is normally quoted as 2.5cm of fish per 4.5 litres. Unfortunately this is not a reliable method as 10cm of small fish (for instance, five neon tetras) is not the same amount of fish as one 10cm gourami. A 10cm gourami will eat more food, produce more waste and use up more oxygen than five neon tetras.

One of the most important factors is the amount of filtration in the aquarium. The better and more efficient your filtration, the more fish you will be able to keep. Never stock your tank to its full capacity as it takes only a very minor accident, such as over-feeding or a pump failure, to kill your fish very quickly. The more fish you have in your tank the higher the chances of disease spreading throughout your fish stocks. When buying your fish, do not allow yourself to be tempted to 'just one more', even to that really nice one you have just seen for the first time. It will end up costing you more when your fish die from overcrowding and you have to replace them. Remember that your fish will grow, so it is always important to leave growing room.

A male swordtail *(Xiphophorus helleri)*. These livebearers are peaceful fish that prefer the middle levels of the aquarium.

TANK SIZE

30- AND 60-LITRE AQUARIA

These are the usual sizes for community tanks. They are large enough for a variety of compatible fish such as mixed livebearers or small characins. Approximately 10 to 20 fish of the usual 2-10cm size can be maintained safely. Beginners are usually successful with mixed livebearers and may find a special advantage in raising swordtails and platies. The hobbyist with too many healthy, colourful fish may be pleasantly surprised to find that a local dealer is often willing to trade these for other fish or for supplies. Guppies are more difficult to dispose of profitably. Many new and colourful varieties of swordtails and platies are now available, including some very attractive high-finned strains.

A lively shoal of checkered barbs *(Capoeta oligolepis)* - a popular species for aquaria.

Most characins, danios and barbs will also do well in tanks of this size. Especially popular are neon and cardinal tetras, head-and-tail-lights, and zebras. Some of the barbs tend to be fin-nippers, and this must be taken into account when mixing species.

This is the smallest size tank suitable for medium-sized cichlids, but here also the individual fish temperament must be considered. Some

TANK SIZE

your first aquarium

This lovely tank won the Best Furnished Trade Aquarium award at the Supreme Festival of Fishkeeping in 1994.

Black or black widow tetra, *(Gymnocorumbus ternetzi)*. The black fades to grey with age.

cichlids are aggressive and bullies; others have a placid disposition with others of their own kind, especially if they are a mated pair. Initial spawning behaviour can be rough, and torn fins are the rule rather than the exception. Angelfish, however, tend to be big bluffers and rarely do serious damage to fish their own size.

LARGER AQUARIA

Almost any variety of tropical fish can be kept in these large tanks, but even here you must guard against the tendency to overcrowd the aquarium. The experienced hobbyist has learnt that a crowded tank is not attractive and that fewer, more carefully-chosen varieties do more to enhance the tank than a helter-skelter mixture of a dozen species of fish paying no attention to one another.

The shape of the aquarium depends on the purpose for which it is intended. Tall, narrow aquaria with large front glass faces are excellent for show but accommodate fewer fish because of the limited surface area available for oxygen and carbon dioxide transfer. Flatter, shallower tanks are best for raising fry and young fish, since they have abundant air surface and swimming room. The standard size aquaria are good for general use. They are also cheaper than the odd shapes and sizes. Tall tanks are especially expensive because of the extra-thick glass required to withstand the greater water pressure at the bottom.

The magnificent angelfish *(Pterophyllum scalare)*.

TEMPERATURE

TEMPERATURE your first aquarium

The usual advice given to beginning hobbyists is to maintain the temperature in tropical fish tanks at 24—25°C. In fact, many fish will do well at somewhat cooler temperatures if these are reached gradually and can be maintained without further sudden drops. Larger amounts of water change temperature very slowly and can be kept at a steady state much more easily than smaller tanks. The 24—25°C range seems to work quite well for the average home aquarium.

THERMOSTAT-HEATER COMBINATIONS

The single unit thermostat-heater is probably the most popular heating device for aquaria. Heaters are available in both non-submersible and submersible types. The latter are more expensive but more easily hidden. They allow each tank to be individually controlled, depending on the variety of fish to be maintained and the condition desired.

SAFETY

This topic can be divided into two parts: safety for the hobbyist and the home, and safety for the fish. Both boil down to the same thing: use good heaters made by respected manufacturers, and use them in accordance with the manufacturers' instructions. Remember to observe all of the safety precautions that come into effect whenever electrical apparatus is used near water.

The submersible thermostat-heater is more expensive than the non-submersible, but it is easier to hide it.

your first aquarium **TEMPERATURE**

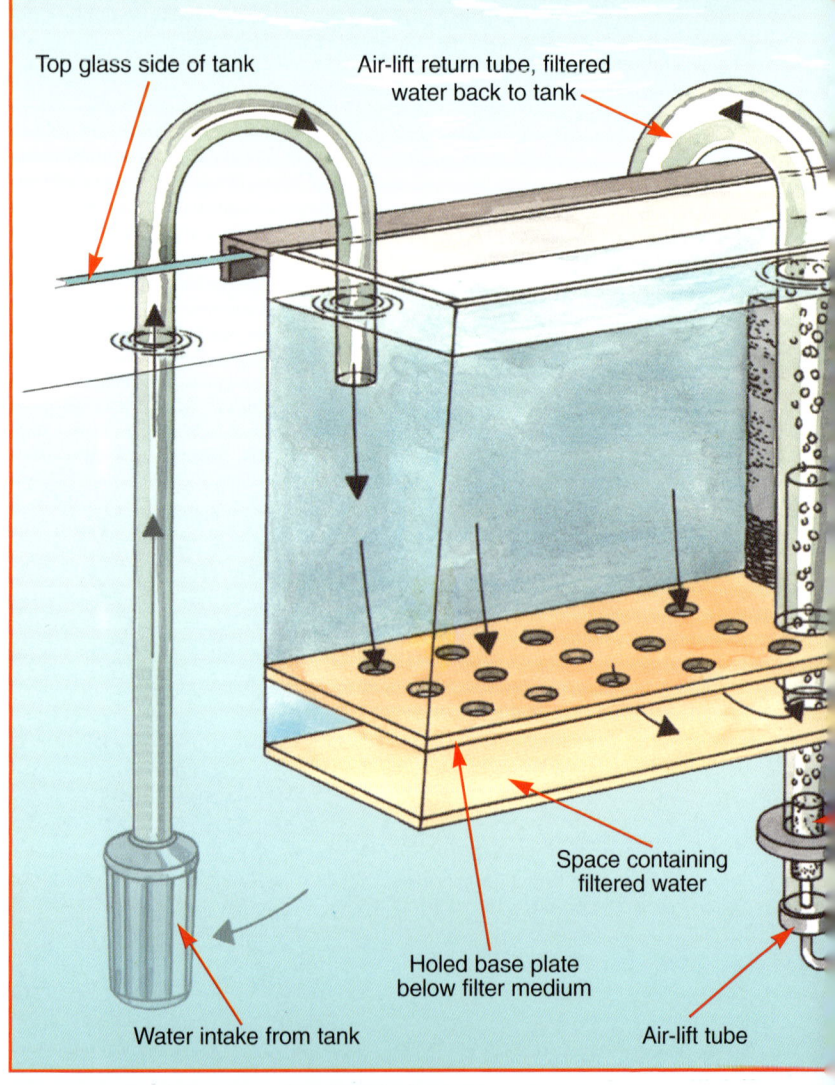

Top glass side of tank
Air-lift return tube, filtered water back to tank
Space containing filtered water
Holed base plate below filter medium
Water intake from tank
Air-lift tube

Cut-away of an external box filter powered by an air pump. Similar filters

AIR PUMPS/FILTERS

AIR PUMPS/FILTERS　　　　　　　　your first aquarium

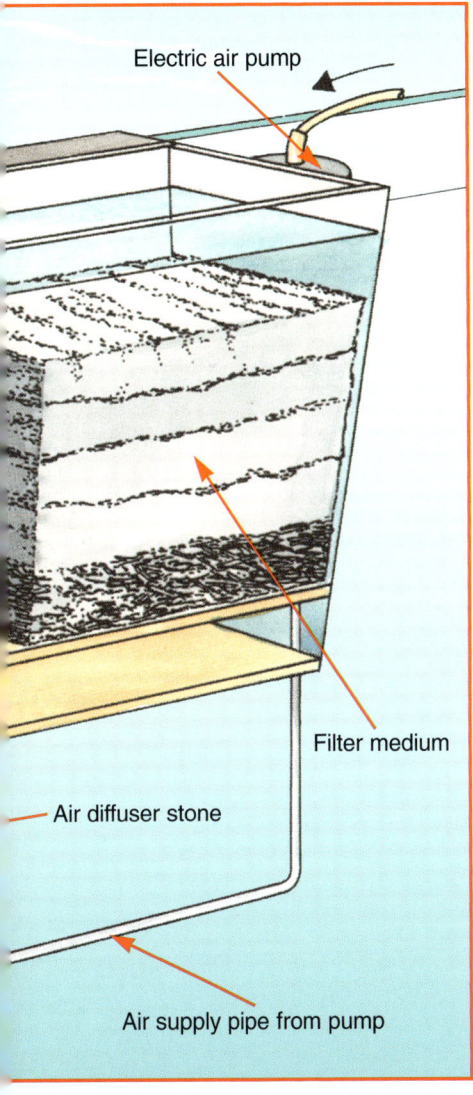

Electric air pump

Filter medium

Air diffuser stone

Air supply pipe from pump

available powered by an electric pump.

Two main types of air pump are used to supply air to filters and air stones. The first is the vibrator type, which is generally smaller and less expensive than the piston type. It comes in various sizes, the smallest vibrator supplying enough air for only one filter or air stone, while the largest can service 18 or more filters.

The air from vibrator pumps is produced under low pressure and exceptionally fine air stones will not be supplied efficiently from this source. The air supply comes from a vibrating diaphragm whose movement depends on the cycles of the alternating electrical current in the home. In the cheaper vibrators this diaphragm is made of rubber and must be replaced periodically, usually annually or when it cracks and leaks. Replacements are available at low cost and easily installed. The smaller, cheaper pumps may have an annoying hum, while the better units are insulated and may be very much quieter.

Piston type pumps produce air under higher pressure and generally produce a larger volume than the vibrators. This pump depends on a standard small electric motor continuously working a small piston and cylinder. It requires periodic maintenance such as oiling the motor, greasing the piston washer, and occasionally replacing the drive belt. Piston pumps are now regarded as old-fashioned and are expensive to buy. Advanced hobbyists with many aquaria, dealers and hatcheries usually need large piston pumps or regular air compressors.

Most hobbyists find that they are most successful in keeping a large aquarium clean and disease-free by using a filter. Several types of aquarium filters are available depending on the circumstances of the individual aquarium. The outside power filter has many advantages. It is very efficient, can be run at high speeds, and is readily accessible for cleaning and for changing the filtering medium. These power filters contain water-moving motors and do not need an air pump. The outside filter is not suitable for a tank containing fry, which may get sucked into the filter intake stem.

The inside corner filter also works efficiently, and provides good aeration, but it must be connected to an air pump to function. It is not as easily accessible for cleaning but, once out of the tank, it is very easy to clean. Most of these are also unsuitable for fry, although some types have such narrow slits for water intake that they may be used in a tank containing even very small babies.

Both of these filters require a filtering medium, which must be replaced periodically. In crowded aquaria this cleaning may have to be done every week. The old stand-by in filtering material is filter floss, which works well and is inexpensive. However, some types have a tendency to mat, which considerably reduces their efficiency.

Undergravel filters are slightly raised, perforated plastic sheets placed on the bottom of the aquarium and covered by the gravel. Air lift tubes are set at the rear corners. They work on a biological principle rather than by the simple mechanical removal of floating debris. These filters create a downward circulation of the aquarium water so that it passes through the gravel on the bottom of the tank to the area below the undergravel filter and is then returned to the surface of the aquarium through the airlift tubes. In the process, any floating debris, such as uneaten food, is deposited in the bottom gravel. The fresh constant supply of oxygenated water passing through the gravel encourages the growth of aerobic (oxygen-loving) bacteria which decompose the waste under controlled conditions and convert waste material into nitrogenous compounds (nitrites and nitrates).

If the filter is run continuously, the water will circulate constantly and the aerobic bacteria will do their job well. If the filter is turned off for more than

AIR PUMPS/FILTERS   your first aquarium

a day or two after it has become well established and after the gravel is loaded with debris and uneaten food, the lack of fresh (oxygenated) water will kill the aerobic bacteria and a culture of anaerobic bacteria which do not require oxygen will rapidly develop and take over. These also use the debris and food in the gravel but tend to produce toxic compounds and gases such as hydrogen sulphide, which gives off the rotten egg odour noticeable in such circumstances. The water can become cloudy and foul-smelling almost overnight.

Aquascaping involves combining plants, fish and other furnishings to their best advantage to make an attractive display.

These filters are also unsuitable for particularly dirty fish such as goldfish, and larger species. Big cichlids with digging habits may also destroy the filter's efficiency by exposing it in an area free of gravel. Some hobbyists have found that the plants do not grow properly in tanks using these filters, possibly because of excess nitrogen compounds in the gravel. Many hobbyists put a sheet of plastic screen between the gravel and the filter itself to prevent individual pieces of gravel from becoming wedged in the filter slots.

The canister filter is also quite popular. Basically this is a cylindrical outside power filter that contains the filtering material. The larger ones support a certain amount of biological filtration as the water flows continuously through them thus providing the needed oxygen. Specially constructed balls or cubes that have increased surface area may also be included in the canister filter to help provide greater biological filtration. The return, as in most power filters, is forcefully sprayed into the tank to provide sufficient aeration for most tanks, along with a little water movement.

The sponge filter is particularly well-adapted for small tanks containing fry. This type filters the water through a block of plastic foam, which removes fine particles without endangering the baby fish. Sponge filters are easy to clean and long lasting.

The angelfish *(Pterophyllum scalare)* is the cichlid most popular with aquarists.

AIR PUMPS/FILTERS
your first aquarium

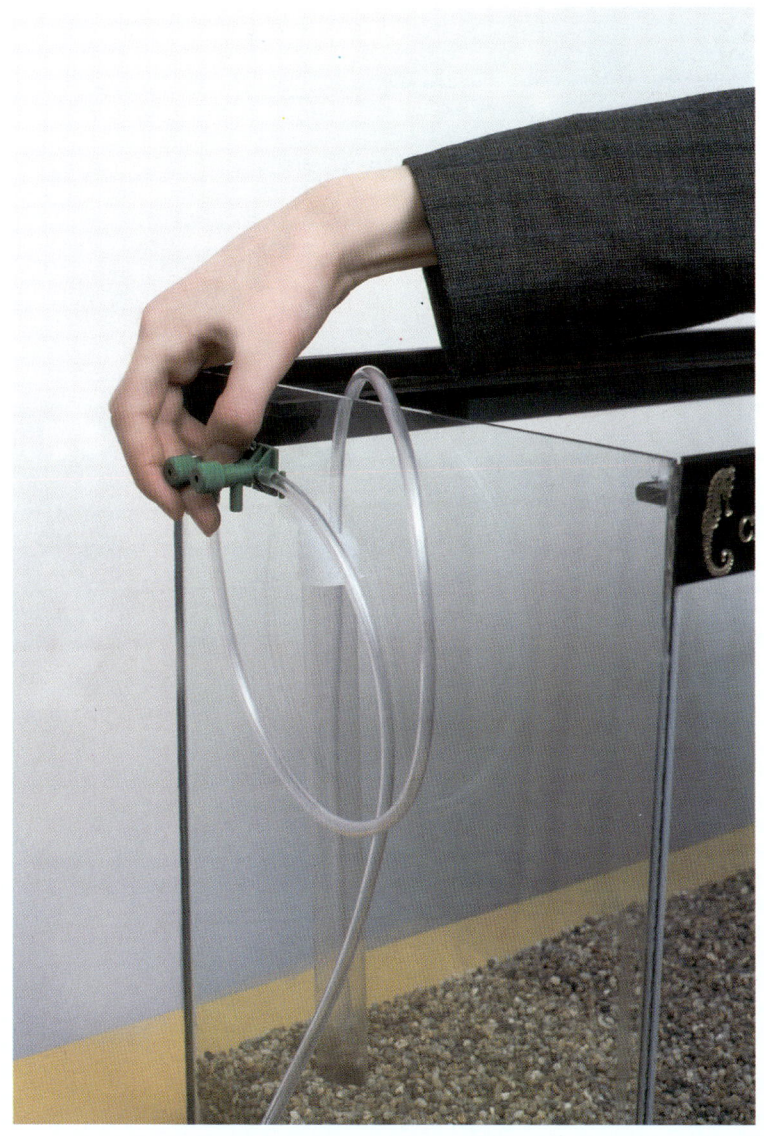

The air supply to an undergravel filter air lift tube is controlled from a plastic control valve which is normally attached to the outside of the tank.

FURNISHINGS

your first aquarium

FURNISHINGS

The number and type of ornaments and rocks suitable for aquarium use is almost endless and largely a matter of individual taste. It is best to buy such things only from aquarium shops unless you have a good knowledge of rocks and can choose those that are safe to keep in your aquarium.

Bogwood is the most frequently used stand-by and is quite safe as well as being attractive and available in a variety of shapes and sizes. It has an additional advantage in that it provides very natural-appearing surroundings, some of the pieces resembling fallen tree trunks and limbs.

Plants make attractive ornaments in an aquarium, and can contribute to the maintenance of healthy conditions. This is water fern (*Azolla filiculoides*).

FURNISHINGS

your first aquarium

Castles and other artificial porcelain or plastic ornaments are safe but provide unnatural-looking surroundings for the fish.

PLANTS

These are the most effective ornaments and they also contribute to the maintenance of healthy conditions in the aquarium. They help to remove nitrogenous wastes (nitrates) from the water and the aquarium gravel but, contrary to popular belief, do not add significant amounts of oxygen to the water. During daylight hours, plants absorb carbon-dioxide from the water and produce oxygen that returns to the water. In the dark, however, the situation is reversed, the plants taking up oxygen from the water and excreting carbon-dioxide, thus cancelling out their previous action.

Congo tetras *(Phenacogrammus interruptus)* darting around among the plants.

Landscaping with plants, as with ornaments and rocks, is largely a matter of personal choice, but certain general rules should be followed. If you want a stable, attractive tank requiring little pruning, avoid rapidly-growing plants such as Indian fern. Slower-growing plants such as the old stand-by, the Amazon sword plant, are better.

your first aquarium — FURNISHINGS

A shoal of rummy-nosed tetras *(Hemigrammus rhodostomus)*.

Long, rush-like plants, such as *Vallisneria* or *Sagittaria*, make a good background in an aquarium and can provide dramatic effects when planted in clumps. These two types of plants, however, do not seem to grow well together. Bushy plants, such as *Anacharis* and *Cabomba*, tend to get spindly and fall apart in aquaria. They are also often nibbled by the fish, and end up looking ragged and untidy. Certain fish, such as various silver dollar species, will eat any kind of plant, so plastic plants are most practical in their tank.

Floating plants can be used to shade the aquarium from bright reflector lights and give a pleasing effect. They may also encourage particularly shy fish, such as dwarf gouramis and some of the dwarf cichlids, to come out of hiding and take an active part in the community tank. Some of these floating plants, such as duckweed, can be annoying and difficult to keep under control, while others, such as Indian fern, are useful for shade and can be kept deliberately as an extra supply of food for the fish. These plants grow rapidly and usually replenish themselves as fast as the fish eat them.

FURNISHINGS   *your first aquarium*

Fish, furnishings and plants, like this eel grass *(Vallisneria spiralis)*, should combine to form an attractive, harmonious whole.

When choosing your plants do consider the amount of light that is available. Most *Cryptocoryne* do well in relatively dim light, while *Vallisneria* or *Sagittaria* require somewhat brighter lighting. Too much light will promote the growth of algae, which may form a thin layer of green growth on the aquarium glass or any surfaces in the tank. Under extreme conditions the water itself may turn a pea-soup green and the fish will be quite difficult to see. If you notice a growth of algae either on the glass or distributed in the water you should cut down either the brightness of aquarium lights or their duration of burning.

GRAVEL

In the usual well-planted aquarium use only enough gravel to provide adequate rooting for the plants. Usually a layer 3—5cm deep is sufficient to provide support for the plants' roots. Too much gravel provides a haven for uncontrolled bacterial growth and hidden food particles that may gradually rot and pollute the water.

Some hobbyists prefer to grow their plants in individual small containers, which they can move around easily to rearrange the aquarium or to catch a particularly fast and wary fish. Under these conditions a layer of gravel thin enough to cover only the bottom is sufficient and will allow the fish to browse completely through it, eliminating any lost food particles.

If an undergravel filter is used, a layer of gravel at least 5cm thick must be used or the filter will not function efficiently.

The usual grade of aquarium gravel is satisfactory for growing most plants and for providing a bottom cover. Fine sand, such as beach sand, packs too tightly and may not allow the plants sufficient root growth, while very coarse gravel or glass or shell fragments provide too many hiding places for fallen debris. The question of natural or coloured gravel is again a matter of personal taste.

Most gravel sold in aquarium shops has been pre-washed but you should rinse it again before adding it to the tank. If you are in doubt about the source, wash the gravel thoroughly in a bucket until the water runs clear.

LIGHTING

LIGHTING
your first aquarium

The aquarium can be placed where it receives indirect daylight but should not be placed directly in front of a window or where it will receive too much direct sunlight; rapid algal growth would be the inevitable result. If such a location is the only one available, give some protection to the aquarium by using paper or another background to cut down the excess outside light. You can maintain better control of the situation if you use artificial lighting. The aquarium reflectors may come wired for incandescent lights, which supply good-quality light for plant growth but, unfortunately, the larger bulbs also supply excessive heat. The top layer of water may become too warm for the comfort of the fish, and water circulation should be maintained with an air stone or filter. Small aquaria will receive sufficient light from a 15- or 25-watt tubular bulb burning six to ten hours daily, depending on the type of plants used for decoration. Larger tanks may require two such bulbs. Most aquaria are too brightly lit, and many shy fish are frightened into darker corners.

Fluorescent reflectors are more expensive than those wired for incandescent light but have the advantage that they supply a cooler light without significantly affecting the water temperature. These are satisfactory for use on the aquarium with the usual daylight or warm white fluorescent bulbs and provide a quality of light adequate for plant growth. They are actually cheaper to maintain, since a fluorescent bulb is more efficient than an incandescent one, giving out more light than an incandescent bulb of the same wattage.

Other types of fluorescent bulb are available, some of which are designed specifically to promote plant growth. They can be used in any fluorescent fixture and give out light predominantly in the red and blue wave lengths. They are not suitable for room lighting and provide a peculiar purple or orchid-coloured tinge to their surroundings. Plant growth depends particularly on these wave lengths, however, and can be spectacular under these bulbs. Fish with significant blue or red colouration, such as neon or cardinal tetras, can appear startlingly brilliant with this type of lighting. Such bulbs are usually not permitted during judging of fish shows because of the colour enhancement achieved.

Aquarium reflectors come in the form of 'full hoods', which cover the entire top of the tank, or 'strip' reflectors, which cover only a small part. The full hoods are more expensive, but offer more protection.

your first aquarium — **LIGHTING**

An aquarium of arresting design, like this one, can be a focal point in your living room. *Photo courtesy of Jan Dirk Van Ginneke.*

LIGHTING

your first aquarium

Above: Congo tetra *(Phenacogrammus interruptus)*
Below: A shoal of neon tetra *(Paracheirodon innesi)*

23

pH AND HARDNESS

The term pH has a complicated scientific definition but for our purposes can be used simply as an indication of the acidity, neutrality or alkalinity of the aquarium water. A pH of 7 is defined as neutral while values below this are acid and above this are alkaline. Most fish can be well maintained in a pH range of between 6 and 7.5, while some are happy only at greater or lesser extremes than these. Most public water supplies are quite all right in this respect, and it is unnecessary to alter the pH for aquarium fish. Your local pet shop will probably be familiar with water conditions in your area and can advise you about what, if any, action you should take.

Once in an aquarium, the water tends to become more acid as it becomes older and more and more waste materials become dissolved in it. This acidification is especially rapid and prominent in a tank with an undergravel filter. In extreme cases the acidity can be corrected using the pH buffers available from your local pet shop, but this should be done slowly over a period of several days if a pH change of more then 0.5 units is to be made.

Extremely alkaline water can be similarly corrected using pH buffers for taking the pH down. pH test kits are easy to use, but the cheap ones have relatively inaccurate printed colour guides. The more expensive test kits come with glass phials containing coloured solutions that can be matched accurately using the usual bromthymol blue indicator dye.

Excessively hard water may be more difficult to overcome. One solution is to dilute extremely hard tap water with either bottled distilled water or the bottled spring water that is generally sold for drinking purposes. Public water supplies in most parts of the country, however, are quite suitable for aquaria. The gradual build-up of excessive hardness because of evaporation and repeated water addition can be overcome by changing 10%-20% of the aquarium water weekly. This will also help prevent the build-up of excess nitrogenous wastes. Hardness test kits and nitrate/nitrite test kits are available at your aquarium dealer and provide a reasonably accurate indication of the condition of your water.

Some hobbyists, once they know the general quality of their water — that is, whether it is hard or soft, acidic or alkaline — try to match the requirements of the fish they keep to the type of water they can provide. They find this easier than trying to change the composition of their water.

FEEDING

Under natural conditions fish browse almost constantly and rarely come upon a large amount of food at one time. In the aquarium too they seem happiest when given several small feeds during the day rather than one large one, part of which may lie uneaten and deteriorating. A good compromise is to feed the fish twice a day, making sure that the second feeding allows enough time for the fish to dispose of all the food before the aquarium lights are turned off.

Dried foods are the staple diet for most aquarium fish. An important factor to consider in choosing a dried food is the percentage of protein it contains. This will be listed on the food container along with the ingredients. The better quality commercial foods contain 30%—40% protein and sometimes more. The amount of protein in poorer quality cereal-type foods may be as low as 5%. Such a large variety of carefully-formulated commercial fish foods is now on the market that you'll have no trouble finding good foods at your pet shop.

Some varieties of fish, such as mollies or scats, need a considerable amount of vegetable material in their diet. Special preparations are available for these fish.

Regardless of the quality of the dried food used, your fish will be healthier and grow faster if their diet also includes some live or frozen foods.

Several types of live foods are available, depending on the season. Live Daphnia (small freshwater crustaceans), bloodworms and Tubifex worms may be obtained from many pet shops. Live adult brine shrimp are sometimes available at pet shops, and brine shrimp eggs are nearly always available. Other live foods that can be bought or raised include earthworms, white worms, and meal worms. Live foods especially adapted for baby fish include microworms and baby brine shrimp. Both of these may be easily raised in the home, providing a ready source of nourishment for fry at any time of the year.

Varieties of frozen foods sold include many of those previously mentioned, Daphnia, bloodworm and brine shrimp being the most commonly available. These seem about equal in nutritional value to the live foods and, in the case of brine shrimp, may be somewhat safer to use, since no living parasites can be introduced into the aquarium water with the food.

your first aquarium   **FEEDING**

The various *Corydoras* catfish are popular aquarium fish and help to keep the bottom of your tank free of uneaten food.

SETTING UP

SETTING UP — your first aquarium

As a beginner, your safest course is to buy a new aquarium from a reputable dealer. The all-glass bonded tanks are virtually leak-proof and quite strong. Rinse out your new tank thoroughly, but do not use any soap or detergent.

A second-hand tank may be contaminated from sick fish previously kept in it, but occasionally you can find a clean used tank which will be a particularly good bargain. You must rinse this out thoroughly and scrub it down inside with a strong salt solution. You can make up a thick paste of moist salt granules to use as a gentle abrasive for more effective cleaning. An older used tank that has stood empty for some time may have dried out and have a tendency to leak. Newer tanks usually are relatively safe in this respect. If you are in doubt, the safest course is to fill the aquarium outside the home to test for leaks before bringing it into the house. A tank should always be empty when it is moved. Tanks are sturdily constructed and strong enough to hold water on a stable base, but are not intended to be lifted or moved when full.

Once you are satisfied that you have a clean, non-leaking aquarium, you can move it to its permanent location. This should be a standard aquarium stand or a sturdy bookcase, table or aquarium shelf. A filled aquarium weighs approximately one kilogramme per litre of water, so a flimsy coffee table or TV stand is not suitable for a large aquarium. If the aquarium shelf is slightly flexible you can give the tank a more stable base by resting it on a slab of polystyrene 2—3cm thick on top of the shelf. Remember also that you are dealing with water; placing an aquarium on a shelf above books or electrical equipment can have disastrous consequences.

Once the tank is in place put in your washed gravel and add the water to within 8cm of the top. You can then have fun landscaping the tank with plants and rocks. If you are not entirely happy about the source of your plants, your aquarium dealer can supply solutions for decontaminating plants and ridding them of any possible parasites or other undesirable organisms. When the landscaping is completed, add water to about 3cm below the top edge and set up the filter and heater-thermostat units.

Let the tank stand overnight to allow chlorine and excess dissolved air to dissipate. Commercial preparations are available from aquarium shops to help dissipate the chlorine quickly. Use these as directed on the container.

your first aquarium　　　　　　　　　　　　　　**SETTING UP**

Your local pet shop will probably be able to supply you with a bacterial culture that will initiate the development of the biological filter. A waiting period of three or more weeks is usually necessary before the nitrogen cycle has stabilised. Your dealer may help you test the water at intervals, or you can do so yourself with a simple test kit.

A male zebra danio *(Brachydanio rerio)***, another small, active shoaling fish.**

SETTING UP your first aquarium

Most fish purchased are placed in plastic bags that can be floated in the warm, filled tank to allow their temperatures to equalise. The fish can then be introduced gently into the aquarium and begin to explore their new surroundings.

It is inevitable that you will occasionally add fish and plants to your new aquarium, but please do your best to control the impulse to do this too often. Sooner or later a new addition will bring in some disease or parasite and then you will be initiated into the more unpleasant side of fish keeping. This is a broad subject and cannot be dealt with here adequately. It is a very good idea to isolate newly-acquired fish in a separate tank for one week before introducing them into the community aquarium.

CHOOSING FISH

You should choose fish for the community tank carefully rather than randomly picking unrelated fish of various types and colours that have nothing in common with each other. Groups of four or five fish of the same type make attractive small shoals and several species can be kept in the same tank if they are of similar size and temperament. All of the various levels in the aquarium can then be used and the general appearance of the tank is enhanced. A group of hatchetfish can be kept for surface fish, and several small shoals of neon tetras, cardinal tetras and zebras can be kept as mid-level fish. An algae eater such as a small *Hypostomus* can complete the population. It will more than earn its keep by keeping the aquarium glass and plants clean. The tank does not require snails; they often prove to be a nuisance and, once introduced, are difficult to get rid of. A single large apple snail is interesting but can pollute the water if it dies in a hidden corner. The following list can be used as a guide to choosing fish for the community tank:

Surface fish: hatchetfish; pearl or gold danios.

Middle levels: most livebearers (also in upper levels); egglaying killifish (also in upper levels); most characins (including neon and cardinal tetras, lemon tetras and rummy-nose tetras); zebra danios; most barbs and rasboras; anabantids (bubblenest builders — the larger types with larger fish only); dwarf cichlids (also in lower levels); larger cichlids (with larger fish only).

Bottom levels: most catfish; clown loaches and other loaches; elephant-nose fish (not for beginners).

your first aquarium　　　　　　　　　　　　　　　**SETTING UP**

A cut-away view of an aquarium showing an undergravel filter in operation.

Lemon tetra *(Hyphessobrycon pulchripinnis).*

SETTING UP

Before I describe in greater detail the different types of fish that the beginner can pick and choose from, I cannot emphasise enough the importance of populating the aquarium slowly. The most common mistake made by the novice is to purchase several fish on the first trip to the aquarium shop. Choosing fish at random often results in instant tank failure. The wide selection of fish available to the hobbyist can be an overwhelming experience for the beginner. Patience is essential and you must select your fish carefully. If you increase the number of fish in your aquarium gradually, and there is no doubt that it will pay off in the long run. Only put hardy fish, such as zebra danios, into your tank before it is fully mature.

There are several beautiful tropical fish suitable for the beginner. Some of the more popular varieties include tetras, livebearers, anabantoids (bubblenest builders), and small catfish. Tetras are small, active fish that require minimal care and prefer to be kept in small shoals. The neon tetra *(Paracheirodon innesi)* and the cardinal tetra *(Paracheirodon axelrodi)* are two popular species. A collection of five or six of these fluorescent beauties moving swiftly around the tank provides a colourful, active aquarium. The rummy-nose and lemon tetras are also desirable species. Although it is virtually impossible to produce ideal conditions for all the different fish in a community tank, a happy medium for the tetras is a clean aquarium with a neutral pH (7.0) and a water temperature of 25-27°C. They eagerly accept dry flake food.

Livebearers are also ideal beginners' fish that work well in the community aquarium. Not only are they easy to care for, but they breed easily in the beginner's tank, and sometimes the newly-dropped fry will hide in plants or ornaments and go unnoticed. Weeks later, the hobbyist has a pleasant surprise when a group of young fish suddenly appears. The most popular livebearer, and one that is highly recognised worldwide, is the fancy guppy *(Poecilia reticulata)*. Fancy guppies are selectively bred to exhibit wonderful colour patterns and long, fancy fins. The livebearers will congregate at both the middle and top layers of the aquarium.

Swordtails and platies are likely to be the beginner's next best choice in the livebearer category. There are numerous incredibly brightly-coloured strains, with reds, oranges, blacks and blues predominating. The male swordtails are easy to distinguish from the females because of their unique sword-like tails and modified anal fins, called *gonopodia*. Both swords and platies are peaceful tank inhabitants. Feeding and providing suitable water requirements can be sustained with relatively little effort.

The smaller anabantoids (bubblenest builders) also make interesting additions to the aquarium. The Siamese fighter is probably one of the best-known anabantoids. The male Siamese fighter's extravagant colour and long, flowing fins make it a desirable and much sought-after species. These fish usually do well in the community aquarium provided they are not mixed with feisty barbs, such as the popular tiger barb *(Capoeta tetrazona)*. Over-aggressive fin-nipping fish will cause tremendous damage to the fins of a slow-moving Siamese fighter. It is called the 'Siamese fighter' because two males put in the same tank will fight furiously, usually to the death, and therefore should never be placed together. Several gourami varieties, including the blue and gold gourami, are relatively peaceful.

Another recommendation for your first aquarium is to include some catfish. Small catfish of the genus *Corydoras* are excellent aquarium scavengers with delightful personalities. They will often eat any leftover food that slips to the bottom of the aquarium, but should also receive their own diet to keep them in the best of health. Corydoras catfish are available in several varieties and will not grow very large in the aquarium. Several of these species can be mixed peacefully with each other, so they are perfect bottom dwellers.

A final suggestion in selecting the first aquarium fish includes the addition of a small algae eater. Since algae eaters need a large vegetarian diet, I suggest that you wait a few weeks until sufficient algae has grown in the newly-established aquarium. If the algae eater is placed in a new tank lacking sufficient algae, it may starve to death. Many fish eat algae and may be considered algae eaters. Most small algae eaters of the genus *Hypostomus* are extremely effective in cleaning algae from the aquarium glass and plants. Although algae is beneficial and an important source of food for many tropical fish, it will become unattractive if allowed to grow excessively.

BIBLIOGRAPHY

SETTING UP AN AQUARIUM
A Complete Introduction
Jim Kelly
ISBN: 0-86622-291-X
CO-003
This book contains all the information that a beginner needs to set up an aquarium and is also useful for the more experienced hobbyist. It covers the types of equipment available and how to use them, which fish and plants to choose, and care and breeding of individual species.
Hardcover: 138mm x 214mm, 128 pages, 52 colour photos and 32 line drawings

COMMUNITY AQUARIUMS
A Complete Introduction
Herbert R Axelrod
ISBN: 0-86622-283-9
CO-013
Dr Axelrod provides useful advice on which species of fish will live together peacefully in a community aquarium, so the hobbyist can avoid trouble in the tank.
Hardcover: 138mm x 214mm, 128 pages, 113 full colour photos and 35 colour line drawings.

SETTING UP AN AQUARIUM
A Step-by-Step Book
Cliff W Emmens
ISBN 0-86622-961-2
SK-033
This easy-to-read book describes the base on which a successful aquarium is built. It provides information in such areas as water quality, fish behaviour, plant needs and purification techniques.
Softcover: 214mm x 136mm, 64 pages, 48 colour photos.

THE NATURAL AQUARIUM
How to Imitate Nature in Your Home
Satoshi Yoshino
Doshin Kobayashi
ISBN: 0-86622-629-X
TS-195
A team of Japanese aquarists has taken the 22 basic designs for aquariums and made them into show tanks. Each design is analysed, fully illustrated and made suitable for the home aquarium.
Hardcover: 260mm x 166mm, 128 pages, illustrated with colour photographs and diagrams.

In this book, the sizes of the aquaria (tanks) are expressed in their capacity in litres. When tanks are sold, however, the size can be described in various different ways, such as litres or gallons; or the dimensions of the tank given in inches or centimetres. The following conversion information may be of help to you in expressing the size of your aquarium in the most convenient terms. When calculating the amount of water your aquarium will hold, do remember that you will not be filling it completely to the top, and allow for the volume taken up by gravel, rocks and other ornaments.

- A litre equals 1000 cubic centimetres or approximately 61 cubic inches.
- One cubic foot holds approximately 28 litres or 6.25 imperial gallons or 7.5 US gallons.
- 1000 cubic inches holds approximately 16 litres or 3.5 imperial gallons or 4.25 US gallons.